A Look at Australia

by Helen Frost

Consulting Editor: Gail Saunders-Smith, Ph.D.

Consultant: Frances Cushing, M.A.
Research Associate
Edward A. Clark Center for Australian Studies
University of Texas
Austin, Texas

Pebble Books

an imprint of Capstone Press
Mankato, Minnesota

Pebble Books are published by Capstone Press
151 Good Counsel Drive, P.O. Box 669, Mankato, Minnesota 56002
http://www.capstone-press.com

1 2 3 4 5 6 07 06 05 04 03 02

Library of Congress Cataloging-in-Publication Data
Frost, Helen, 1949–
    A look at Australia / by Helen Frost.
    p. cm.—(Our world)
    Includes bibliographical references and index.
    Summary: Simple text and photographs depict the land, animals, and people
of Australia.
    ISBN 0-7368-1165-6
    1. Australia—Juvenile literature. [1. Australia.] I. Title. II. Series.
DU96 .F76 2002
994—dc21
                                                 2001003423

The author thanks the children's section staff at Allen County Public Library in
Fort Wayne, Indiana, for research assistance.

Note to Parents and Teachers

The Our World series supports national social studies standards related to culture. This book describes and illustrates the land, animals, and people of Australia. The photographs support early readers in understanding the text. The repetition of words and phrases helps early readers learn new words. This book also introduces early readers to subject-specific vocabulary words, which are defined in the Words to Know section. Early readers may need assistance to read some words and to use the Table of Contents, Words to Know, Read More, Internet Sites, and Index/Word List sections of the book.

Table of Contents

Australia

Canberra
★

Australia is a large island country. The island also is a continent. The capital of Australia is Canberra.

Australia's flag

Outback

mountains

rain forest

beach

6

The middle part of
Australia is called the
Outback. Most of the land
there is flat and dry.
Australia also has mountains,
rain forests, and beaches.

kangaroo

koala

8

Kangaroos hop through the Outback. Koalas live in trees in Australia.

More than 19 million people live in Australia. Most Australians live in cities near the coasts. Sydney is Australia's largest city. English is the official language of Australia.

Aborigines have lived
in Australia for more
than 50,000 years.
Most Aborigines now
live in cities. Some
still live in the Outback.

Many Australians play Australian rules football. They also play rugby, soccer, and tennis. Surfing and swimming are popular in Australia.

16

Farmers grow grapes and wheat to earn money. Australians also raise sheep and cattle. Workers use steel to make cars.

Australia's money is counted in Australian dollars.

18

Australians travel by train, bus, car, and airplane. Small airplanes bring supplies to the Outback.

Australia's Great Barrier Reef is the longest coral reef in the world. People go diving to see the coral and the fish that live there.

Words to Know

Aborigines—the first people to live in Australia; many Aboriginal stories and songs tell about the land and animals.

Australian rules football—a version of football that is a mixture of soccer and rugby; players use an oval ball and play on an oval field.

continent—one of the seven large land masses of Earth; Australia is the smallest continent.

coral reef—a type of land made up of the hardened skeletons of corals; corals are small sea creatures that are many colors.

island—land surrounded by water; Australia is an island; Australia is a little smaller than the continental United States.

Outback—the remote, interior part of Australia; the Outback is made up of deserts and plateaus.

rugby—a form of football played by two teams; players kick, pass, or carry an oval ball.

Read More

Berendes, Mary. *Australia.* Faces and Places. Chanhassen, Minn.: Child's World, 1999.

North, Peter, and Susan McKay. *Welcome to Australia.* Welcome to My Country. Milwaukee: Gareth Stevens Publishing, 1999.

Petersen, David. *Australia.* A True Book. New York: Children's Press, 1998.

Pluckrose, Henry. *Australia.* Picture a Country. New York: Franklin Watts, 1999.

Internet Sites

Australia: The Land and Its People
http://www.webweaver.com.au/australia/index.html

The World Factbook 2000—Australia
http://www.odci.gov/cia/publications/factbook/geos/as.html

Zoom School: Australia
http://www.enchantedlearning.com/school/Australia/index.html

Index/Word List

Aborigines, 13
airplane, 19
beaches, 7
bus, 19
Canberra, 5
car, 17, 19
cattle, 17
cities, 11, 13
coasts, 11
continent, 5
coral, 21

English, 11
farmers, 17
Great Barrier
  Reef, 21
island, 5
kangaroos, 9
koalas, 9
money, 17
mountains, 7
Outback, 7, 9,
  13, 19

people, 11, 21
rain forests, 7
sheep, 17
steel, 17
surfing, 15
Sydney, 11
train, 19
wheat, 17

Word Count: 185
Early-Intervention Level: 17

Editorial Credits
Mari C. Schuh, editor; Kia Bielke, cover designer; Jennifer Schonborn, production
  designer and illustrator; Kimberly Danger and Alta Schaffer, photo researchers

Photo Credits
Bill Bachman, cover
CORBIS, 16; Eye Ubiquitous, 12 (left)
Digital Stock, 8 (both), 18
International Stock/Frank Grant, 14
Michele Burgess, 6 (upper left)
PhotoDisc, Inc., 1
Photo Network/Larry Dunmire, 20
Trip/Eric Smith, 6 (upper right); J. Dennis, 6 (bottom right)
Unicorn Stock Photos/Tommy Dodson, 10; Frank Pennington, 12 (right)
Visuals Unlimited/Will Trover, 6 (bottom right); David B. Fleetham, 20 (inset)